TEACHER'S HANDBOOK

GOODBYE RAINBOW

Songs for students of English as a foreign language

Ken Wilson & Keith Morrow

Longman

LONGMAN GROUP LTD.
London

Associated companies, branches, and representatives throughout the world.

© Ken Wilson 1975

All rights reserved. No part of this publication may be reproduced, stored in a retrieval system, or transmitted in any form or by any means, electronic, mechanical, photocopying, recording, or otherwise, without prior permission of the Copyright owner.

First published 1975
Sixth impression 1980

ISBN 0 582 52483 0

Printed in Hong Kong by
Commonwealth Printing Press Ltd

Contents

	Introduction	5
1	City Boy *get used to/be used to*	8
2	Looking forward to the day *phrasal verbs etc.*	12
3	The houses are built *present simple passive/ past simple passive*	16
4	One day *simple past tense*	21
5	Questions *questions*	25
6	He'd still be here *conditionals*	28
7	Goodbye Rainbow *adverbs of frequency and manner*	32
8	Nothing has changed *everything, -one, -where, nothing, no one, etc.*	36
9	Not enough ways *too much/too many, too . . . to do (something), not enough, so much, so little*	40
10	Seagull *relatives*	44
11	Glitter hair-cream *comparatives and superlatives*	49
12	Along the road *prepositions*	53

Introduction

The use of songs in the teaching of English is no longer regarded as a gimmick or a device to while away an empty Friday afternoon. Songs are now recognised as an extremely flexible aid, and experience has shown that they not only provide students with motivation to learn but can also be used to improve actual language performance.

This booklet has been written to accompany a new collection of songs called *Goodbye Rainbow*. The songs have been written and recorded by The Solid British Hat Band, who produced *Mister Monday*, and both the songs themselves and these notes have been greatly influenced by the experience gained from using the first collection and from talking to other teachers about improvements they would like to see.

As in *Mister Monday*, each song concentrates on a particular language area which is likely to cause problems for foreign learners of English, but in contrast to the earlier collection these songs lay much more stress on the inherent theme or story which is presented. The themes have been deliberately chosen to appeal to a generation accustomed to taking an interested and often critical look at the world around them. They are not 'protest' songs, but at the same time they go beyond the blandness of some of the earlier material and raise issues which are recognisably of the 1970s.

When and How to Use these Songs

The great merit of using songs for language teaching is their adaptability. Many teachers will want to use these songs in their own way for their own purposes. The following are merely suggestions.

When

1 *Introducing new language points*

A typical language/grammar lesson will have three stages:

  i Presentation of new language form(s) in suitable situations.

  ii Drilling/Reinforcement.

  iii Development of the forms leading to their use in new situations.

The songs may be used at any stage of the lesson, but experience has shown that their chief value lies in the reinforcement and development stages rather than for initial presentation. The suggested exploitation of the songs in this book assumes that the class already has a *passive* knowledge of the grammatical features covered, and aims at helping to make this passive knowledge *active*.

2 *The Remedial Lesson*

It follows that songs provide useful material for remedial work, especially when a student may resist more conventional remedial techniques, having already failed to learn in this way.

3 *The Conversation/Discussion Lesson*

The presentation of a theme through a song can lead to immediate discussion if the class is familiar enough with the language of the song to be able to understand it without difficulty.

In what follows, Sections 1–6 are designed for those using the songs as reinforcement/development of new language forms, or remedial work. Teachers using the songs purely as a basis for discussion should first check in Section 1 that the language of the song will be reasonably familiar; then concentrate on Sections 2 and 6.

How

Each song is dealt with under six headings:

1 *Language Features*

This is a check-list of the language/grammar points occurring in the song. There is also a vocabulary section, listing the less well-known words and providing explanations of words and idioms where this may be helpful.

Some teachers find it useful to present most, if not all, the new vocabulary of a song before playing it to the class, but it is also possible to combine the explanation of vocabulary with step 3 (see below).

2 *Immediate Class Involvement*

Our aim at this stage is to focus the class's attention on the song from the first moment. In many cases the words will not be fully understood at the first hearing, so concentrate instead on a reaction to the *music*. Ask the class if they like the tune. What does it make them think of? Would it be possible to dance to the music? What instruments can they hear? How would they judge the mood of the song? etc. If it is likely that enough of the song has been understood at the first hearing, ask the class what they think the title might be.

In all cases, encourage discussion and help the class to express their ideas.

3 Establishing the Words

The words of each song are given on the relevant page. Here are two suggestions for communicating them to the class.

i Write up each verse on the board with a number of words left blank (approximately one per line). Play the verse to the class; ask them to provide the missing words orally and then to copy the verse down.

ii Play each verse a line at a time and ask individuals to repeat each line after you have played it. After a whole verse has been repeated, either write it on the board and ask the class to copy it down or use the song as a dictation: play the verse and ask the students to write down the words as they listen.

4 Understanding the Song

A number of comprehension questions are given for each song, together with suitable replies. The latter are not the only possible correct answers in many cases, and should be treated simply as guidance.

5 Exploitation of Language Features

Suggestions are given for development and oral practice work, based on the language features practised in the song.

6 Relation of Song to Personal Experience

This final section is a 'transfer' section, in which the students are given an opportunity to use the language of the song creatively, relating the ideas and opinions in the song to their own situation and experience.

City Boy

Chorus:
　　I'm a city boy from the centre of town,
　　I'm used to seeing the rain come down,
　　I'm a city boy and I like being free,
　　And living in the country isn't for me.

1. I can't get used to the quiet at night,
   I can't get used to the fields.
   I'm used to artificial light
   And the moon in the sky looks real.

Chorus:
　　I'm a city boy etc.

2. I can't get used to the fresh-faced girls
   Or the smell of flowers on the air.
   I'm used to eating food from tins
   And seeing motor cars everywhere.

Chorus:
　　I'm a city boy etc.

3. I'll never get used to waking up
   And hearing the birds in the trees.
   I'll never get used to them singing
   Or to the humming of the bees.

Chorus:
　　I'm a city boy etc.

4. But I'm going to get used to walking
   And smiling at the passers-by.
   Oh, country life is the life for me,
   I'm going to kiss the city goodbye.

Coda:
> I'm getting used to the country
> And I'm getting used to the trees.
> I used to like the city lights
> And now I love the birds and bees.
>
> He's getting used to the country
> And he's getting used to the trees.
> He used to like the city lights,
> Now he loves the birds and bees.

Language Features

to	be / get	used to	seeing . . . the quiet at night.

Vocabulary

Chorus (the country) isn't for me (i.e. I don't like the country, it doesn't suit me);
Verse 1 artificial light (i.e. electricity, neon lights);
Verse 2 fresh-faced (= bright, healthy-looking; in this context implies: not wearing make-up);
Verse 3 the humming of the bees; to kiss the city goodbye (i.e. say goodbye to the city);
Verse 4 passers-by.

Immediate Class Involvement. See Introduction (page 6).

Establishing the Words. See Introduction (page 7).

Understanding the Song

A Say if the following statements are true or false according to the song. Make corrections where necessary.
1 There's a lot of smoke in the country.
2 At first, the singer prefers the country to the city.
3 He's used to noise, so he doesn't like the quiet of the country.
4 Girls in the country use more make-up than city girls.
5 The country air smells different from city air.
6 He isn't used to eating fresh food. etc.

B Ask the following questions:
1 What sort of weather does the singer like?
   He likes rain. | rainy / wet | weather.
2 Why can't he get used to the moon?
   It | seems / looks | real and he is used to artificial light.

3 What is the difference between the girls in the country and the ones the singer is used to?
   In the city the girls wear | *make-up.*
                                | *cosmetics.*
4 What other things does he miss in the country?
   He misses food from tins and motor cars.
5 What does he think about hearing birds in the trees?
   He thinks it is very strange.
6 What does he make up his mind to do?
   He makes up his mind to get used to walking and smiling at | *people.*
                                                                | *passers-by.*
   etc.

Exploitation of Language Forms

A Collect examples of the different uses of *be/get used to* in the song:
1 I'm used to seeing the rain come down/artificial light. etc.
2 I can't get used to the quiet at night/the fields. etc.
3 I'll never get used to waking up/hearing the birds in the trees. etc.
4 I'm going to get used to walking/smiling at the passers-by.
5 I'm/He's getting used to the country/trees.

B Look at each in turn:
1 Ask: Why is he used to . . . ?
   Establish: He was born and grew up in the city.
   Develop this theme by asking questions about other things people are used to in a city and then about people in different professions, jobs, e.g.
       What is a farmer (teacher, bus driver, factory worker, nurse, etc.) used to?
       Possible answers include: working hard, getting up early, working in a noisy atmosphere (a lot of noise), looking after sick people, routine, etc.
2 Ask: Why can't he get used to . . . ?
   Establish: Because it seems strange/it's new to him.
   Develop: Write the following replies on the blackboard:
       a) Yes, I'm used to/getting used to it/them.
       b) (No, but) I'll get used to it/them.
       c) (No,) I can't/I'll never get used to it/them.
   Prepare, or get the students to prepare questions which will elicit any of these answers, or variations using the forms already practised, e.g.
       Do you enjoy coming to these classes?
       Do you enjoy working with children? (if possible, choose something appropriate to each student's work) etc.

3 Ask: Why does he say this? What does it tell us about his intentions?
   Establish: He | is determined | to get used to these things.
              | has made up his mind |
4 Ask: Has he been successful?
   Establish: Not completely yet, but things are getting better.
   Practise: Some sentences from (ii) in this form. Set the scene by asking the class to imagine the singer three months later.

Relation of the Song to Personal Experience

Two possible developments suggest themselves:

1 Town vs. Country
   Ask your class if there is a great difference between country life and life in the town in their country. What sort of differences may exist? Why? What advantages and disadvantages can the students see in town and country life?
2 Adapting to a new Environment
   Ask if any member of the class has ever been in the position of having to adjust to a new way of life, like the singer. Most will have had at least the experience of moving to a new school or job, and many will know the problems of moving to a new city or country. How long did it take them to get used to the new situation? In which aspects have they succeeded/failed?

Looking forward to the day

Chorus:
    So listen to their words and look at their faces,
    Are they going to wipe out our wide open spaces?
    Think about the noise you have to put up with,
    Is this the way you want your children to live?

1. I'm looking forward to the day
   When everybody can stand and say:
   You can't get away with that!
   If you take out, you must put back,
   Help us to save our skies and seas
   And don't let them cut down all our
       trees.

2. It's time to stand up for what you feel,
   To make sure that what they say is real.
   Find out what they really mean
   Is it what you have often seen?
   What they invent turns out to be
   The ruin of our society.
   Chorus:
       So listen etc.

3. I'm looking foward to the day
   When I see the clouds all roll away.
   If the aeroplanes don't fly
   We can make out the blue in the sky.
   Let's live the simple life again
   And learn to get on with other men.
   Chorus:
       So listen etc.

Language Features
Phrasal and Prepositional Verbs

a)	Phrasal Verbs (Verbs + Adverbial particles)	take out put back cut down find out	turn out wipe out roll away make out
b)	Verbs + Prepositions	listen to look at	think about
c)	Phrasal–Prepositional Verbs	look forward to get away with stand up for	put up with get on with

The distinction between phrasal verbs and prepositional verbs is complex, and many different ways of analysing them have been suggested. For the purposes of studying them within the context of this song, two features should be pointed out:

1. the particle of a phrasal verb can often stand either *before or after* a noun, but only *after* a pronoun, e.g.
   Don't *cut down* all our trees.
   Or: Don't *cut* all our trees *down*.
   But: Don't *cut* them *down*.
2. the parts of a phrasal verb (verb + particle) can often be replaced by a single-word verb; also, the meaning of the combined parts often cannot be found by looking at the literal meaning of the separate parts:
   find out (verse 2) = discover; *turns out* to be (verse 2) = proves to be, becomes in the end; *wipe out* (chorus) = destroy; *make out* (verse 3) = see, distinguish.

Vocabulary

Verse 1 get away with (that) = succeed in doing (that) without being punished, blamed;
Verse 2 stand up for (someone/something) = defend;
Verse 3 put up with (someone/something) = endure;
Verse 4 get on with (someone) = live or work together in harmony (see also phrasal verbs in *b* above).

Immediate Class Involvement. See Introduction (page 6).

Establishing the Words. See Introduction (page 7).

13

Understanding the Song

A Say if the following statements are true or false according to the song. Make corrections where necessary.
1 The singer is looking forward to the day when people will defend what they believe in.
2 People are destructive.
3 The singer wants to preserve open spaces.
4 She likes a lot of noise.
5 She wants life to be different for her children.
6 Getting on with people is more important than inventing new machines.
etc.

B Ask the following questions:
1 Does the singer want the future to be like the past?
   No, she wants to change the way we live.
2 If nobody helps her, what does she say will happen?
   The skies and seas will be polluted and the trees will be cut down.
3 What is the effect of new inventions?
   They | destroy | our society.
   * | ruin |*
4 What are "wide open spaces"?
   Country where nothing has been built, where the effect of Man cannot be seen.
5 Is the singer concerned only with this generation?
   No, she is thinking about the way our children will live.
6 What effect does she think planes have on the sky?
   She thinks they | make it dark. |
   * | pollute it. | etc.*

Exploitation of Language Forms

A Work through the song with the class, drawing their attention to how the verbs are used and, where necessary, to what they mean. Discuss alternative ways of expressing (as closely as possible) the same thing, e.g.
   I'm *looking forward to* the day . . . : I'm thinking about the time . . .
   You *can't get away with* that: You won't succeed in doing that/If you do that, you'll be punished
   (It) *turns out* to be the ruin . . . : It ends up by being the ruin/by ruining . . .

B Take each verb in turn and see if the class can suggest other words or phrases which might be used with it to fit in with the theme of the song. Here are various suggestions, but encourage the class to make their own wherever possible.

1 You can't get away with *that/polluting the world/destroying the environment.*
2 It's time to stand up for what you *feel/think is important/believe (in).*
3 Find out *what they really mean/what the truth really is/what lies behind their words.*
4 ... turns out to be *the ruin of our society/the end of our world/the means of destroying our way of life.*
5 I see *the clouds* all roll away/*darkness/black dirty clouds/smoke.*
6 ... learn to get on with *other men/our fellow men/each other.*

Relation of the Song to Personal Experience

The general theme of the song (the importance of the conservation of nature and the dangers of industrialisation) will probably be recognised by most students. How relevant are they to your particular city or country?

Two particular lines from the song may lead to discussion:
1 What they invent turns out to be/The ruin of our society.
>Can the class think of any examples of this? e.g. the motor car:
>What are the advantages and disadvantages of the increasing use of cars?
>What conclusions can be drawn?
2 Let's live the simple life again ...
>Is this a realistic or even a desirable aim? What is the "simple life"? What advantages/drawbacks does it have?

The houses are built

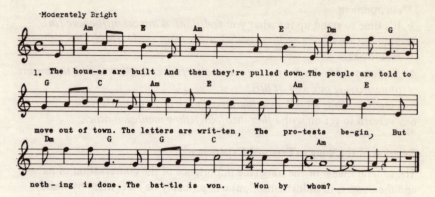

1. The houses are built
   And then they're pulled down.
   The people are told to move out of town.
   The letters are written,
   The protests begin,
   But nothing is done.
   The battle is won.
   Won by whom?

2. A motorway is needed,
   We must start right away.
   A thousand trees are cut down the very first day.
   An election is held,
   The other party wins –
   And the very next day
   The motorway begins.
   Built by whom?

3. A church is demolished,
   The protest is faint,
   The office block's named after a very famous saint.
   The offices are damaged
   By an accidental fire.
   A hymn of thanksgiving
   Is sung by the choir.
   Nothing's changed.

4. A minister's invited to open a road,
   A traffic jam delays him
   And the day is wet and cold.
   Several of the guests
   Are taken down with flu,
   The minister arrives
   And catches it too.
   Down with flu.

5. A man was accused
   Of anti-social deeds:
   He tried to stop the motorway rolling on his weeds.
   The case was defended,
   But the prosecutor won –
   Everyone was happy
   For justice was done.

Language Features

Passives

present	The houses are built Nothing is done
past	A man was accused

Vocabulary

Verse 1 protests;
Verse 2 motorway, right away (= immediately), election, (political) party;
Verse 3 to demolish, faint (= weak), office block, to damage, accidental, hymn of thanksgiving, choir;
Verse 4 traffic jam, to be taken down with flu (catch/go down with influenza);
Verse 5 to be accused of . . . , anti-social deeds, to roll, weed(s), (legal) case, to defend, prosecutor, justice.

Immediate Class Involvement. See Introduction (page 6)

Establishing the Words. See Introduction (page 7)

Understanding the Song

A Say if the following statements are true or false according to the song. Make corrections where necessary.

1 People write letters because they want a motorway.
2 Trees are cut down to make way for the road.
3 The party that wins the election is against a motorway.
4 A church is built to replace the office block.
5 Everyone is very angry when the church is pulled down.
6 A man is taken to court for protesting about the motorway.

B Ask the following questions:

1 What are the people told to do when their houses are pulled down?
   They are told to | move out of | their town.
   | leave |
2 How do the people protest about what has happened?
   They write letters./They protest by writing letters.
3 What is the result of their protests?
   Nothing happens./Their protests are in vain.
4 The "other party" wins the election. How many parties are there and what do they stand for (or against)?

17

There are two parties: the party that wins the election wants the motorway; the other one is against it.
5 What is built when the church has been demolished?
An office block is built | *to replace* | *the church.*
　　　　　　　　　　　　 | *instead of* |
6 Why is the minister late when he opens the road?
Because he is | *delayed* | *by a traffic-jam.*
　　　　　　　　 | *held up* |

C

1 Discuss the effect in the song of the following lines:
　　a) Won by whom? (v. 1)
　　b) Built by whom? (v. 2)
　　c) Nothing has changed. (v. 3)
　　d) Everyone was happy/For justice was done. (v. 5) Justice for whom?
2 What is the point of verse 4?
　(irony? anti-climax?)

Exploitation of Language Forms

Point out that in this song the passive is used without any agents (by + (pro)noun), since the singer is concerned with the action and result rather than the 'nameless force' causing the action. Note how the 'namelessness' of the agent adds to the sense of helplessness in the song: if we know who is hurting us we can perhaps do something about it; if we don't know, we always feel frustrated.

A

1 Ask questions with *who*.
　　e.g. *Who tells the people to move out of town?*
　　　　 Who wins the battle?
　　　　 Who needs a motorway?
　　　　 Who demolishes the church? etc.
Establish: We don't know./The song doesn't tell us.
(Have we any idea who is responsible?)
2 Ask questions with *when*.
　　e.g. *When are the people told to move out of town?*
　　　　 When are the letters written?
　　　　 When is the battle won? etc.
Establish: We don't know exactly. It has happened in the past sometimes; it is happening today; it will probably happen again in the future. It is happening all the time.

3   Ask questions using *when* about the last verse.
    e.g.   *When was the man accused?*
           When was the case defended? etc.
    Establish: As above we don't know exactly, but now we are talking about one particular event which happened in the past.
    (Does it matter *when* it happened? Could it be happening today?)

This unexpected use of the past tense focuses our attention on the "man", since he was the only one that *did* something; the others are always content merely to talk or write letters. Note also that we would expect an adverb of past time here, and its omission adds to the effect of 'timelessness' of the song: the man's protest might merit a newspaper headline for one day, but no one would remember when or why he made it.

B   Retell the story of the song in the past tense.
1   Supply suitable adverb prompts to fix the events at a definite time in the past.
    e.g.   *yesterday/last week/last month/six months ago/before the holidays* etc.
2   Give one of these per verse and ask the class in turn to retell one line of the song to fit the new situation.
    e.g.   *Last month* — The people were told to ...
                          The letters were written ...
           Last year — A motorway was needed.
                          We had to start right away.

Note the different effect produced by using an adverb of definite past time; it seems now that people want to remember the details of each event and record them.

Relation of the Song to Personal Experience

Of the five verses, four lend themselves to discussion by posing basic problems: e.g.
1   Is the rapid development and rebuilding of cities always desirable?
2   Which are most important, roads or trees? Is the conservation of nature more important than 'progress'?
3   How effective can an individual/a group of individuals be when their way of life is threatened by 'the march of progress'? Will there be room for 'individuals' in the future?

In every case the class can be invited to comment and, where appropriate, to provide examples from their experience or from 'mythology'. E.g. for verse 5 every country has its national heroes or martyrs who took a personal stand against oppression. This may be the basis for future work leading perhaps to the acting out of the story of the hero/martyr by one group for the rest of the class.

One day

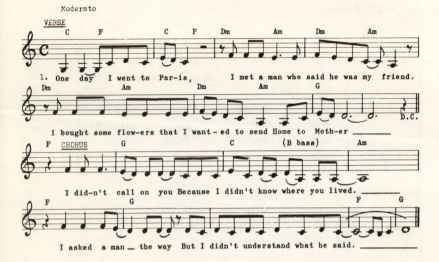

Chorus:
I didn't call on you
Because I didn't know where you lived.
I asked a man the way
But I didn't understand what he said.

1. One day I went to Paris,
   I met a man who said he was my friend.
   I bought some flowers that I wanted to send
   Home to Mother . . . .

2. One day I flew to London,
   I saw some people walking in the park.
   I took a picture of the palace in the dark
   And the sunset. . . .

   Chorus:
   I didn't call on you etc.

3. One day I sailed to Mexico,
   I ate some chili and then I drank some wine.
   I lay on the beach and thought that it was fine
   In the sunshine. . . .

   Chorus:
   I didn't call on you etc.

4. Yesterday I came back home again,
   I turned the key and opened my front door.
   I didn't want to travel any more
   Until next time. . . .

   Chorus:
   I didn't call on you etc.

Language Features

Past simple forms

Affirmative

Regular	/id/ want*ed* /t/ ask*ed*	/d/ liv*ed* sail*ed*	turn*ed* open*ed*	
Irregular	went met said was	bought flew saw	took ate drank	lay thought came

Negative

I didn't	call know	understand want

Vocabulary

Chorus   call on you (= visit you; cf. call you = telephone you);
Verse 3 chili (= a favourite Mexican food made with chilis).

Immediate Class Involvement. See Introduction (page 6).

Establishing the Words. See Introduction (page 7).

Understanding the Song

A Say if the following statements are true or false according to the song. Make corrections where necessary.
1 First the singer went to Rome.
2 She bought some flowers for a friend.
3 Then she went to London by train.
4 She painted a picture of Buckingham Palace.
5 She went to Mexico by ship.
6 It was cold there. etc.

B Ask the following questions:
1 Who did she meet in Paris?
   She met a | stranger | who said he was her friend.
            | man |
2 How did she get to London?
   She went by | air. | She caught a plane.
               | plane. |

3 What did she try to do there?
   She tried to visit a friend's house, but couldn't find the way.
4 What time of day did she take a photograph of the palace?
   She took the photograph | in the evening.
   * | as the sun was going down.*
   * | (at dusk).*
5 Did she fly to Mexico?
   No, she didn't. She went by | sea.
   * | ship.*
6 What did she do there after her meal?
   She lay on the beach sunbathing. etc.

Exploitation of Language Forms

A Work through the song line by line and, wherever possible, ask one member of the class to ask a question, to which the line of the song could be the reply. Another member of the class should give the reply.

    e.g. A: Where did she go one day?
            B: She went to Paris.
            C: Who did she meet there?
            D: She met a man.   etc.

After doing this for the first two verses, allow the class to make up questions referring to any part of the song.

B Get the class to 'invent' stories or short narratives. Make three columns, A B C, on the blackboard, using verbs/places in the song and any others you may like to practise,

	A (verbs)	B (places)	C (verbs)
e.g.	went	London	met
	flew	Paris	saw
	sailed	a desert island	found
	swam	the moon	bought
	etc.	etc.	etc.

Ask a student to make a sentence using a verb + place from columns A and B with a suitable adverb of past time. Then the next student will continue, taking a verb from column C, and so on, each student adding verbs they like. As soon as one story 'dries up', start a new one. The stories can be improbable, e.g.

    Ten years ago my uncle went to the moon and discovered a mountain of solid gold.

This could be done in groups, with two or three 'neutral' students acting as judges of the most original or most amusing story.

Relation of the Song to Personal Experience

Ask if anyone in the class has been to the places mentioned in the song. If so, what did they see and do there?

What makes a perfect holiday? Has anybody ever been anywhere that has seemed perfect?

This could lead to written follow-up work if you ask the class to write a travel feature describing a place they have visited or would like to visit. (N.B. If a student is writing about a place he would like to visit, tell him to use the past simple tense and describe what happened as if he had been there in a dream.)

Questions

1. Do you know the answers to my questions?
   Can you help me find the reason why?
   Are you trying to understand me?
   Or will I never know?

2. Where are we going and what are we doing?
   Why are we lying and who are we fooling now?

3. Do you understand when people talk to you?
   Do you think that what they say is true?
   Do you find that life's confusing?
   Or will I never know?

4. Why do people never mean what they say?
   Why do I always see the rain . . . every day?
   Where does the sun go when it sets at night?
   Why do we wake up in the morning light?

5. Did you hear me when I called you?
   Did you want to give a helping hand?
   Were you there or were you hiding?
   Will I never know?

6. What did I do to make you go away?
   How did I hurt you, what did I say . . . yesterday?
   Where did the clouds come from to fill the skies?
   Where did the love go that I used to see in your eyes?

Coda:
   Will I never know? etc.

Language Features

Questions forms:

present (simple, continuous); past (simple, continuous); future (will).

a) *Yes/No questions* i) with *do*	Do you know the answers? Did you hear me?
ii) with aux. vbs + inversion	Can you help me? Are you trying to understand me? Were you hiding?
b) Question words (*who/what/where/why/how*)	Where are we going? How did I hurt you?

Vocabulary

Verse 2   to fool someone (colloquial, = to deceive someone);
Verse 5   to give someone a helping hand (or: give someone a hand, = help someone).

Immediate Class Involvement. See Introduction (page 6).

Establishing the Words. See Introduction (page 7).

Understanding the Song

Ask the following questions:

1. Who's she singing to?
   Her | ex-boy friend *(who used to love her but has now left her)*.
       | ex-fiancée. *(He has broken off the engagement.)*
2. What does she think about life and the way people live?
   Life is pointless. People deceive (cheat) each other.
3. Does she find it easy to get on with other people? Why?
   No, she doesn't. She doesn't understand or trust what they say and she is confused.
4. How would you describe her state of mind?
   Confused/full of doubts.
5. Why did he leave her?
   Because she hurt his/hurt his feelings.
6. What is her life like now he has gone?
   Empty/sad/full of sorrow. (Her world has crumbled around her.) etc.

Exploitation of Language Forms

A Look in turn at each question posed by the song. Keeping the question form fixed, ask the class if they can suggest different ways of completing the question without changing the meaning completely:

    e.g. (verse 1)   1 Do you know *the way/how to answer my questions*?
                         2 Can you help me *discover the truth/understand the world*?
                         3 Are you trying to *help me*?
                         4 Or, will I never *learn/find the answers*?

It is important that the students should be encouraged to produce questions of their own and to discuss together any slight differences in meaning between the original and their questions.

B Give clues and get each student to ask pairs of questions:

    e.g.   T: You can help me.   T: I understand English.
            S: Can I help you?   S: Do you understand English?
            T: How – ?   T: How well – ?
            S: How can I help you?   S: How well do you understand English?   etc.

Relation of the Song to Personal Experience

Ask the class if they ever feel, or can remember feeling themselves the sentiments expressed in the song. If they seem unwilling to talk of their personal experiences, they might be able to give some examples from books they have read or films they have seen, especially about problems of growing-up and coming to terms with life and love.

Discussion topic

State the proposition: The sentiments in this song would probably be considered by older people to be 'typical of adolescence'.

Question: Does everyone over 40 become cynical, or are the young naïve?

He'd still be here

Chorus:
    If I had told him that I needed him,
    He wouldn't have run away.
    If I had told him he meant the world to me,
    He'd still be here today.

1. When we met each other we were young,
   If we'd been older who can say?
   We would have known the way to talk
      to each other
   And he'd still be here today.

2. I got angry when he was late,
   I never asked the reason why.
   If I'd given him the chance to tell me
      his story,
   He wouldn't have had to lie.

   Chorus:

3. If I hadn't been so cruel,
   He would have told me what was wrong.
   I would have seen that he needed love
      from me
   And I wouldn't be singing this song.

   Chorus:

4. But the day came and he left
   If I'd called him, he would have stayed.
   Now he's far away and he's gone
      forever
   But the memory will never fade.

   Chorus:

Language Features

Conditional Sentences

| If we'd been older | we would have known ... |
| If I'd told him ... | he'd still be here today. |

Vocabulary

Chorus   He meant the world = He was extremely important to me.
           (I thought the world of him.);
Verse 4 The memory will never fade = I will never forget him.

Immediate Class Involvement. See Introduction (page 6).

Establishing the Words. See Introduction (page 7).

Understanding the Song

A Say if the following statements are true or false according to the song. Make corrections where necessary.

1 They were too old when they met.
2 She was angry when he was late.
3 She never asked him why he was late.
4 She lied to him.
5 She told him that she needed him.
6 She left him. etc.

B Ask the following questions:

1 What age were the couple when they met?
   They were young.
2 What problem did this cause?
   They didn't know how to talk to each other.
3 What happened when he was late?
   She got angry but never asked why.
4 Why did he have to lie to her?
   Because she wouldn't give him the chance to explain the truth.
5 What did he really need from her?
   He really needed love.
6 What would have happened if she had called him?
   He | would have stayed with her.
      | wouldn't have left her.

Exploitation of Language Forms

A Draw the attention of the class to the main language feature: conditionals. Point out that these are all 'unreal' conditions: the *if*-clause refers to the past and the action is always unfulfilled The verb form after *if* is *had + past participle*:

> If we'd been older ... (but we weren't)
> If I'd given him the chance ... (but I didn't)
> If I'd told him ... (but I didn't)

The other half of the sentence may refer either to the past (verb form: *would have + past participle*) or to the present (verb form: *would + infinitive*).

Pick out examples from the song. Say the first half of the sentence and ask the students to complete it, saying whether the second half refers to the past or the present:

> T: If we'd been older,   S1 we would have known ...
> (but we didn't — past)
> T: If we'd been older,   S2 he'd still be here today.
> (but he isn't — present)

B The singer here is indulging in 'wishful thinking' (I wish I had told him — but I didn't) and regret (her understanding of the situation has come too late). Develop this idea of 'regret' within the context of the song. Introduce the phrase 'It's a pity' and ask the students to supply sentences on this pattern (note the use of the simple past tense):

> It's a pity they weren't older when they met.
> It's a pity she got angry/didn't ask him why he was late.

Then ask *Why?* and the students reply:

> Because if they'd been older, they'd have known how to ...
> or: Because then they'd have known how to ...

C When the structure is being used correctly and fluently within the context of the song, begin to relate it to the students' own experience, e.g.

> T: What did you do last night?
> S: I went to the cinema.
> T: What would you have done if you hadn't gone to the cinema?
> S: I'd have stayed at home/read a book/watched television, etc.

Get the students to prepare and ask each other similar questions:

> S1 Did you go to see a film last week?
> S2 No, I didn't have time.
> S1 If you'd had time, which film would you have gone to see? etc.

Relation of the Song to Personal Experience

1 Ask the students to talk about missed opportunities or regrets they may have.
2 After some general expressions of the students' experience, try to involve them in the situation of the song. What would they have done? Why? What result would they have hoped for?
3 Ask them to imagine they are talking to the singer
    a) before her boy went away: they suggest what she *should do*;
    b) after he has gone away: they suggest what she *should have done*.
4 A follow-up exercise could take the form of a reply from the 'Problem Page' of a magazine. The students first compose a letter asking for advice in a situation similar to that in the song; then they write the reply.

Goodbye Rainbow

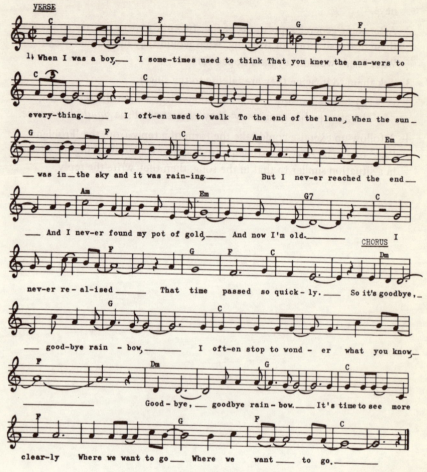

Chorus:
So it's goodbye, goodbye rainbow,
I often stop to wonder what you know;
Goodbye, goodbye rainbow.
It's time to see more clearly
Where we want to go
Where we want to go.

1. When I was a boy,
   I sometimes used to think
   That you knew the answers to
      everything.
   I often used to walk
   To the end of the lane,
   When the sun was in the sky and it was
      raining.
   But I never reached the end
   And I never found my pot of gold,
   And now I'm old.
   I never realised
   That time passed so quickly.

Chorus:
   So it's goodbye, goodbye rainbow etc.

2. Now that I'm a man,
   I hardly ever think
   About the times I spent so happily.
   And I can sometimes see
   A reflection of me
   In the child who sits and plays so
      quietly.
   Life will always be the same —
   And I hope she'll never feel the pain —
   It's just a game.
   I never realised
   That time passed so quickly.

Chorus:
   So it's goodbye, goodbye rainbow etc.

3. Don't try to live too fast
   Or you'll end up living in the past.
   Don't try too hard.
   Most people usually find
   They rarely remember the bad times.

Chorus:
   So it's goodbye, goodbye rainbow etc.

Language Features

Adverbs

Adverbs of time (frequency)	sometimes often never	hardly ever always	usually rarely
Adverbs of manner	(more) clearly happily	quietly quickly	
	fast	hard	

Vocabulary

Title and Chorus the expression 'follow the rainbow' is used for someone who is chasing ideals or dreams which are impossible to realise, just as it is impossible to find the end of the rainbow (i.e. the 'pot of gold');

Verse 1 lane = a quiet road in the country,
pot of gold: according to tradition, if you follow a rainbow to its end you will find a pot of gold there;

Verse 2   reflection of me: the singer sees a child who reminds him of how he used to be;
pain: here = sorrow, sadness;
Verse 3   to end up (doing something): after trying many things, you finally do something you don't want to do because there is nothing else you can do!

Immediate Class Involvement. See Introduction (page 6).

Establishing the Words. See Introduction (page 7).

Understanding the Song

A Say if the following statements are true or false according to the song. Make corrections where necessary.

1 "You" in the first verse refers to the rainbow.
2 When the singer was a boy, he used to try to follow the rainbow.
3 He found his pot of gold at the end of the lane.
4 Time passes slowly.
5 His child reminds him of his own youth.
6 We would all be happier if we took life more easily. etc.

B Ask the following questions:

1 What did the singer often do when he was young?
   He often used to go for a walk to try to follow a rainbow.
2 What was he looking for?
   He was looking for the end of the rainbow, and the pot of gold.
3 What does he now realise?
   He realises that time passes much quicker than he thought.
4 Does he often think about his youth now?
   No. He hardly ever/rarely thinks about it.
5 What does he think when he sees his daughter?
   She makes him think of his youth. He realises life will always be the same.
6 What do most people usually remember?
   They usually remember the good times of their life.

Exploitation of Language Forms

A Pick out from the song examples of the use of adverbs of frequency. Notice the position: (before the verb) I *often* used to think . . . ; I sometimes used to walk . . . ; I never reached . . . (after an auxiliary or modal) I can *sometimes* see . . . ; life will *always* be the same.

1 Ask questions about the song. The students answer using one of the adverbs in the song:

    T: When the singer was a boy, did he think about the rainbow?
    S: Yes, he often used to think/thought about it.

2 Divide the class into pairs or groups. Ask them to prepare questions which they can ask each other individually or as a group. They can use any tense and any adverb of frequency (*ever* will be useful in questions):

    Do you often/ever get up at 6 o'clock — No, I never/Yes, I always get up . . .
    Have you ever been to the seaside? — Yes, I always go to the seaside for my holidays.

B Write a list of common 'action' verbs on the board. Ask the students to make short sentences with these, seeing how many different adverbs of manner can be used with each verb (allow only 'sensible' sentences):

    e.g. speak: quickly, fast, slowly, clearly, well, badly, etc.
          work: fast, hard, slowly, well, badly, quietly, efficiently, etc.

Relation of the Song to Personal Experience

Is it true, in the experience of the class, that young people are more idealistic than adults? Why is this? Can they think of any examples from real life or literature/films? Can they see any changes in their own outlook during the course of their life? Can they themselves "see clearly where they want to go"?

Nothing has changed

Chorus:
    Nothing has changed in this town since you've gone.
    Nothing has changed and nothing gets done.
    No one has moved in this town since you've gone.
    Nothing has changed but nowhere's the same.

1. Everywhere I go
   People seem so slow.
   Everything I do
   Brings back memories of you.
   Everyone I see
   Seems to be looking at me.
   Everytime I open my door,
   I feel I can't take any more.

   Chorus:
   Nothing has changed etc.

2. Something inside me
   Tells me I was a fool.
   Somewhere in the big wide world
   You're thinking that too.
   Someone should have told me
   What I had to do.
   Some time in the future
   I'm going to get to you.

   Chorus:
   Nothing has changed etc.

3. I don't need anybody
   To tell me I was wrong.
   I haven't got anything to do
   The days are getting long.
   There isn't anywhere
   I can call my home.
   So please call me any time
   You can be sure that I'll come.

   Chorus:
   Nothing has changed etc.

Language Features

Every, Some, Any, No in compounds

EVERY	-where -thing -one

ANY	-where -thing -body

SOME	-where -thing -one

NO	-where -thing -one

Vocabulary

Verse 1   (it) brings back memories of you = (it) reminds me of you/makes me think of you,
I can't take any more = I can't bear/stand any more;

Verse 2   I'm going to get to you = I'm going to reach you (either physically or mentally). Note that both 'reach' and 'get (through) to' can be used in the sense of 'make (someone) understand', e.g. We all tried to persuade him to agree, but none of us could reach him (i.e. we could not make him understand our reasons).

Immediate Class Involvement. See Introduction (page 6).

Establishing the Words. See Introduction (page 7).

Understanding the Song

The following statements are all false. Find the words in the song which show that they are not true.

1. The singer always sees busy, active people.
   Everywhere I go people seem so slow.
2. He has managed to forget the girl he used to love.
   Everything I do brings back memories of you.
3. The town has been completely modernised since she left.
   Nothing has changed in this town since you've gone.
4. Important things are being done in the town.
   Nothing gets done.
5. He didn't require advice from anyone.
   Someone should have told me what I had to do.
6. His days are always full. He is never bored.
   I haven't got anything to do. The days are getting long.

Exploitation of Language Forms

Collect together with the class references from the song to:

      1 Place   2 Things   3 People   4 Time e.g.

1. Everywhere I go people seem slow.
   Somewhere in the big wide world you're thinking that too.
   There isn't anywhere I can call my home.
   Nowhere's the same.
2. Everything I do brings back memories of you.
   Nothing has changed in this town since you've gone.
   Something inside me tells me I was a fool.
   I haven't got anything to do.
3. Everyone I see seems to be looking at me.
   No one has moved in this town since you've gone.
   Someone should have told me what I had to do.
   I don't need anybody to tell me I was wrong.
4. Every time I open my door, I feel I can't take any more.
   Some time in the future I'm going to get to you.
   So please call me any time.

Keeping the *some/any/every/no* part of these sentences fixed, ask the class if they can provide any other ways of finishing the sentence to fit the general theme of the song.

    e.g.   Everywhere I go I see people who remind me of you.
                                 I keep thinking of you.
                                 the world seems different without you.
                                 people seem to have changed. etc.

It may be necessary at first to provide prompts:

    e.g.   Everywhere I go see people/remind me/you.
                                 keep/think/you.
                                 world/different/without you.
                                 people/changed. etc.

But this type of exercise is most useful if the class are encouraged to make their own responses, within the context of the song.

Relation of the Song to Personal Experience

Discuss with the class the meaning of the line:

    "Nothing has changed but nowhere's the same".

Have they themselves ever had this feeling, perhaps on returning to a place they knew as children or on meeting again someone they used to know?

Is the singer right to feel as he does? What advice would the class give him? Should he forget the girl and find someone new or is it worth waiting and hoping?

How would the girl feel if she heard this song? Would she be moved by the boy's feelings or would she think that he was being pathetic and weak?

Not enough ways

Chorus:
    There are not enough ways to help each other,
    Not enough ways to care.
    Too many people taking too much of the little we have to share. . . .

1. There are too many people and there's too much noise,
   There are too many cars on our roads.
   We are building too much on our beautiful land
   For the people the cities can't hold.

2. The children of the rich have too many toys,
   But the children of the poor have none.
   It's time to change the way we live
   And give a little to everyone.

    Chorus:
        There are not enough ways to help
           each other etc.

3. The rich are too lazy to give up their cars
   The poor are too hungry to fight.
   They say we're too young to know what is wrong
   We're too young to say what is right.

   Chorus:
   There are not enough ways to help each other etc.

4. I've got so much to say but there's so little time,
   Perhaps it's too late to begin.
   There isn't much hope for our children
   If we can't love our fellow men.

   Chorus:
   There are not enough ways to help each other etc.

Language Features

Quantifiers

too much (noise)	too many (people)
not much (hope)	
so little (time)	not enough (ways/time)

too + adjective + to-infinitive

the rich			lazy to give up . . .
the poor	are	too	hungry to fight
we			young to say . . .

Vocabulary

Verse 4   fellow men: 'fellow' used attributively, as here, = of the same kind, associated together, e.g. fellow travellers = people travelling together.

Immediate Class Involvement. See Introduction (page 6).

Establishing the Words. See Introduction (page 7).

Understanding the Song

A   Say if the following statements are true or false according to the song. Make corrections where necessary.
1 Our cities are overcrowded.
2 We aren't building enough in the countryside.
3 We must give all the toys to poor children.
4 Poor people are too lazy to fight.

5 Older people are always ready to listen to younger people.
6 There's plenty of time to put things right. etc.

B Ask the following question:
1 Describe the places the singer tells us about in line one.
   Too many people; overcrowded/overpopulated (population explosion).
   Too much noise; noise is overpowering/deafening (gets on your nerves).
2 Why must we build so much?
   The cities must expand to make room for all the people.
3 Why does the singer use the example of toys to show the difference between the rich and poor children?
   Toys are a luxury. The poor cannot afford luxuries. (Rich children are spoilt.)
4 Can the poor fight for their rights?
   No. They're too hungry. (They're starving.)
5 Do older people think that the young have the right answers?
   No. Older people say they're too young/inexperienced/immature.
6 What must we do to give hope to our children?
   We must learn to love each other/get on with our fellow men/live in peace and harmony.

Exploitation of Language Forms

Ask the students to pick out examples of the use of *too much, too many, not enough, a little, so little, so much, too + adjective.*

Arrange these in groups, adding words (where necessary) to show the complete structure, etc.

1 There are *too many people* (in our cities).
  There is *too much noise* (in our towns).
  There isn't *much hope* (for our children). etc.
2 We are building *too much.*
  (They) are taking *too much.* etc.
3 There aren't *enough ways* (to help each other).
  There's *so little time* (to say everything). etc.
  (cf. There's too little time to say . . .)
      There isn't enough time to say . . .)
4 The rich are *too lazy* (to give up their cars).
  We're *too young* (to know what is wrong).
  It's *too late* (to begin). etc.

A Ask students to suggest other words which might be used in these examples, either extending the meaning of the original or adding to it, e.g.

There are too many people; there is too much noise: Our cities are overcrowded — there aren't enough houses; there's too much traffic (e.g. cars, lorries, juggernauts, etc.); there's too much smoke (i.e. air pollution), etc.
Too many people (are) taking too much . . .: a lot of people are selfish and greedy; 'The more one has the more one wants'; not enough people are willing to share . . . , etc.

B Take each group in turn and practise them in questions and answers. Encourage the students to ask as well as answer questions, using *too much, enough*, etc. Begin by referring to the song and then transfer to the students' own interests, etc.

    e.g. 1 Why is there too much noise in our cities?
           Because there's too much traffic/there are too many cars.
        2 Why are we building too/so much in the countryside?
           Because there's not enough room (to build any more) in the towns. etc.

(transfer)
        3 Why don't you walk to school/work?
           Because it's too far/I'm too lazy. etc.

Relation of the Song to Personal Experience

1 Ask the class to say what parts of the song they agree or disagree with and why.
2 It is a 'protest' song, but it puts forward no practical solutions. Can anyone make some suggestions?
3 Ask the students how they imagine life in the future. Have they read any books or seen any films describing life in the future? To what extent do these seem
    a) possible and good
    b) possible and desirable
    c) totally unrealistic.

Seagull

1. A free man is a man
   Who can wake up and smile in the morning.
   A poor man is a man who can die
   Without any warning.
   We are the ones who want to be free,
   They are the ones who say what we must be.

2. A friend is a man
   I can go to when I'm feeling down.
   An enemy's a man
   I don't want to see around.
   We are the ones who want to be free,
   They are the ones who say what we must be.

3. A flower is something that blossoms in the spring.
   A tree is something that makes me want to sing.
   A seagull is a bird that flies near the sea,
   An owl is a bird that's wise – wiser than me.

4. A pen is something I use
   To write down what I feel:
   A building is something they make out of concrete and steel.
   A song is something you sing to the trees,
   The wind is something that tells you – if you are free.

Language Features

Relatives

a) *who/that* as subject	a man who can smile something that blossoms
b) omission of *who(m)/that* as object	someone (whom/that) I can go to a pen is something (that) I use

Articles

a) *a/an*	an owl is a bird
b) *the*	the sea, the wind sing to the trees
c) omission	concrete and steel

Vocabulary

Verse 1   warning (n);
Verse 2   to feel down (= to feel depressed, miserable); to see someone around (= see him in any place);
Verse 3   to blossom; seagull; owl;
Verse 4   concrete; steel.

Immediate Class Involvement. See Introduction (page 6).

Establishing the Words. See Introduction (page 7).

Understanding the Song

A Say if the following statements are true or false according to the song. Make corrections where necessary.

1 A free man is a man who can die without any warning.
2 A friend is someone I don't want to see around.
3 An enemy is someone I always want to see.
4 Flowers blossom in the winter.
5 Trees make me feel happy.
6 A seagull is a bird that flies in the mountains. etc.

B Ask the following questions:
1 What is the difference between a free man and a poor man?
   A free man can be happy/enjoy life.
   A poor man may die at any moment. (He has nothing to smile about.)
2 The song says people "want to be free". What is stopping them?
   "They" always try to tell you what to do.
3 Who are "they"?
   The people in | power. |
   * | authority. |*
4 Why is it good to have a friend?
   A friend can help you when you are feeling | down. |
   * | depressed. |*
5 What happens to flowers in the spring?
   They | blossom/bloom. |
   * | come out. |*
6 What does the singer use a pen for?
   He uses a pen to | write down what he feels. | etc.
   * | express his feelings in writing.|*

Exploitation of Language Forms

A Collect a list of all the definitions in the song and arrange them into six sets:

1 A free man is a man who ...
   A poor man is a man who ...

2 We are the ones who ...
   They are the ones who ...

3 A flower is something that ...
   A tree is something that ...
   The wind is something that ...

4 A seagull is a bird that ...
   An owl is a bird that ...

5 A friend is a man I can go to ...
   An enemy is a man I don't want to ...

6 A pen is something I use ...
   A building is something they make ...
   A song is something you sing ...

Now ask the class to provide their own definitions by completing the sentences above in their own words.

B Use the same sets of patterns:
1 To describe occupations.
   Ask: *What's a butcher/teacher/doctor/dentist.* etc.
   Establish: *A butcher's a man who sells meat.* etc.
2 To distinguish two people or two groups of people.
   Make up and act out mini-dialogues; e.g.

Hotel Receptionist: *Are you the gentleman/lady/people who phoned yesterday?*
Man/Woman: *No. I'm/We're the one(s) who phoned last week.*

Substitute time phrases: *this morning/last month/on Tuesday*, etc.
Substitute situations: *travel agent/customer(s)/wanting to go to different countries*
Substitute verbs: *made enquiries/arrived/lost your passport*, etc.

3 To define an inanimate object in terms of something that it does.
Ask: *What's a camera/computer/lighthouse/clock*, etc.
Establish: *A camera is something that takes photographs*, etc.

4 To define an animal or insect in terms of something that it does or with special characteristics.
Ask: *What is a bee?*
Establish: *A bee is an insect that makes honey/buzzes/lives in a hive.*
Substitute animals: *cow (animal/give milk, eats grass)*
 monkey (lives in trees, eats fruits)
 spider (insect/spins a web)
 mosquito (insect/bites people) etc.

5 To show the relationship between another person and the speaker.
Practise again the items in 1 above.

 e.g. *A butcher is a man I buy meat from.* etc.

6 To show how the speaker makes use of things.
Practise again suitable items in 3 above.

 e.g. *A camera is something I/we/you use to take photographs*, etc.

Note: a) In general definitions of this kind we often use "*you*" (= "one"), as in the last two lines of the song.
 b) Short definitions may require the use of a preposition, e.g. (We write with a pen) A pen is something we/you write *with*.

Relation of the Song to Personal Experience

1 Discuss the title of this song, i.e. What is the underlying theme? Why is it called "Seagull"? Is it an appropriate title? Get the students to give reasons. They may be able to suggest other titles, in which case they should explain why they prefer their title to the original.

2 We associate spring with flowers; owls with wisdom (why?); the wind with freedom (why?). What other similar associations

 a) are common in any given society
 b) have students formed for themselves from their personal experience.

Discuss these.

3 Ask the class to give examples from their own experience (as children, teenagers and/or adults) of occasions when they have felt their freedom to be restricted by the opinions or actions of others. When are such restrictions necessary, inevitable, unacceptable, etc.

4 An advanced class might like to comment on the 'them and us' view of society and give opinions on
    a) to what extent is this (un)avoidable and/or
    b) what can be done to reduce the tensions it creates.

1. I used to be a little man
   But I'm much taller now.
   You can be a happier person
   And I can show you how.

2. Be a better looking man
   Use new Glitter hair-cream.
   Glitter will make you look much smarter
   Than you've ever dreamed.

3. Healthier hair makes you feel better
And all the others feel worse.
You'll be the most attractive man
Because you found it first.

4. The richest men in England
All use Glitter hair-cream.
The most successful pop stars
Say Glitter makes all the girls scream.

5. Glitter will make you the best in the world
At anything you choose.
You'll be the fastest racing driver
And you'll never lose.

6. So go round to your local shop
And ask the man for Glitter.
It's better, richer and it's cheaper
Than a pint of bitter.

So buy some Glitter today!

Language Features

Comparative and superlative adjectives

Regular	(much) taller/happier the most attractive the fastest
Irregular	better worse the best

Vocabulary

Verse 1   to glitter (= to shine brightly with flashes of light, like stars);
Verse 2   good-looking; hair cream; smart;
Verse 3   attractive;
Verse 4   pop star; to scream;
Verse 5   racing driver;
Verse 6   bitter (= a type of English beer).

Immediate Class Involvement. See Introduction (page 6).

Establishing the Words. See Introduction (page 7).

Understanding the Song

A Say if the following statements are true or false according to the song. Make corrections where necessary.

1 The singer is taller than he used to be.
2 If you use Glitter, you will feel happier.
3 Only rich men use Glitter.
4 Girls scream when pop stars use Glitter.
5 They scream because they don't like Glitter.
6 You'll never be a good racing driver if you use Glitter. etc.

B Ask the following questions:
1 How has Glitter changed the singer?
   He used to be | little | but now he's much taller.
   * | small |*
2 What does the singer say he can show you?
   He can show you how to be | happier.
   * | a happier person.*
3 What will happen if you use Glitter hair-cream?
   You will look much smarter (that you've ever dreamed).
4 How do you feel with healthier hair? How do others feel when they see you?
   You feel better. Others feel worse.
5 What will you be if you find Glitter first?
   You'll be the most attractive man in the | class.
   * | town.*
   * | country. | etc.*
6 Why do pop stars like Glitter?
   It makes all | the girls | scream.
   * | their fans | etc.*

Exploitation of Language Forms

1 Collect a list of the comparative forms used in the song (i.e. adjectives ending in *-er*): taller/happier/better/smarter/healthier/(worse)/richer/cheaper

   a) Ask: *Why should men use Glitter?*
      Establish: *It'll make them taller/happier*, etc. (as above).
   b) Extend to: *It'll make them feel (look) taller/happier*, etc.
   c) Ask the class if they have ever seen advertisements using promises like the ones made in the song. What sort of words do they use? Can they give examples using the Glitter framework?

2 a) Act out mini-dialogues: e.g.
      X: *My girlfriend says I'm too weak. What can I do?*
      Y: *Use Glitter! It'll make you (feel) stronger.*
                                    (look)
   or X: *My boyfriend's too weak. What can I do?*
      Y: *Tell him to use Glitter! It'll make him . . .*
   b) Show how it is possible to use the superlative form in the above responses, e.g.
      Y: *Use Glitter! It'll make you (feel/look) the strongest man in the world.*
      Practise this using all the adjectives used earlier.

Relation of the Song to Personal Experience

The song can be used to introduce a study of advertising and advertisements at various levels of sophistication.

1 At a simple level, students may be asked to collect examples of advertisements from newspapers and magazines (preferably, but not necessarily in English). Discuss with the class what the advertisement is about and whether it is likely to be successful.

2 More advanced students might like to classify advertisements into various types and say how each aims to achieve its desired effect. They could also discuss advertising media: which are the most/least effective (newspapers, magazines, bill-boards, radio, television, etc.).

3 At the highest level, students might discuss the ethics of advertising. Does it manipulate people's minds (i.e. to what extent do people become 'brainwashed')? To what extent do advertisements exaggerate or even tell lies? Is this permissible/wrong?

Along the road

Chorus:
> They're always right behind you,
> And they're watching from above,
> They're everywhere around,
> They're turning you upside down – upside down.

1. I used to live in a city
   Next to an urban motorway.
   From my bedroom window
   I couldn't see the light of day.
   One day they came into my room
   And said I had to leave,
   Now I'm on the road to freedom
   And a place where I can breathe.
   I'm with a lot of people
   We're living under the sky,
   We've seen right through the games
       they play
   And the tricks we've seen them try.

Chorus: They're always right behind you etc.

2. Along the road to freedom
   There's a place where we can stay.
   There's sunlight in the garden
   We can let the children play
   Those who are destroying us
   Will have to stay outside.
   The people who believe in us
   Can come inside and hide.

Chorus:
   They're always right behind you etc.

3. Beyond that range of mountains
   Is where we're heading for.
   We've been travelling along this road
   For a thousand miles or more.
   We can't live in the city
   And we can't fish in the sea,
   But you can travel beside me
   To build a new community.

   Chorus:
       They're always right behind you etc.

Language Features

Prepositions and adverbs

> in, next to, from, into, with, under,
> through, behind, above, around, along,
> outside, inside, beyond, beside

Vocabulary

Verse 1 urban (= of the town) motorway; on the road to (= on the way to, travelling towards); to see through someone/someone's tricks (= not to be deceived by ...);

Chorus right behind you (= immediately behind you); to turn someone/something upside down (literally: to turn so that the top is at the bottom; here: to confuse. Note another expression: 'I don't know whether I'm standing on my head or my heels ' = I'm completely confused);

Verse 2 to believe in someone (= trust, have trust in someone; cf. to believe someone);

Verse 3 range of mountains; to head for ... (= go towards, in the direction of).

Immediate Class Involvement. See Introduction (page 6).

Establishing the Words. See Introduction (page 7).

Understanding the Song

A Say if the following statements are true or false according to the song. Make corrections where necessary.

1 The singer used to live in the country.
2 His room was very light and sunny.
3 He left because he wanted to.

    4 He's on his own now.
    5 They're living in the open air.
    6 They want to stay this side of the mountains. etc.

B Ask the following questions:
1 Describe the place where the singer used to live.
    It was noisy and dark/gloomy/depressing.
2 What did the singer do when ordered to leave?
    He left the city to find freedom/a better life.
3 Where is he living now?
    He's living in the country/in the open air.
4 What does he hope to find?
    He hopes to find a place where | *he can settle down.*
                                            | *there is room to breathe.*
                                            | *the children can play.*
5 There are two types of people in the world. What does the singer say they do?
    One group is destroying freedom. (He wants to escape from them).
    The other group shares the singer's ideas/beliefs/ideals.
6 What do the singer and his friends aim to do?
    They aim/intend to build a new community/world/life.

Exploitation of Language Forms

A Pick out prepositions and adverbs   i) with a literal meaning   ii) with an idiomatic meaning.
    Write them in lists on the board.

i) a) *live IN a city*   Q: Where else can people live?
                                  A: In a town, in the country, in the mountains, etc.
                                  (extend: in a house, in a flat, etc.)

   b) *I'm WITH a lot* Write the sentence: *Yesterday* I went *to the cinema*
      of people   with *a friend.*
                          Substitute the words in italics, e.g.

                                  the other day/to the seaside/my family
                                  this morning/for a walk/my dog

   c) *They're turning* Have suitable objects available, e.g. a glass, cup, box, etc.
      you UPSIDE   Ask individual students to place the objects in certain
      DOWN   positions as you tell them. Then get the students to tell
                                each other, e.g.

                                  Turn the glass upside down. Now turn it up the right way again.
                                  Put the box on its side. Now turn it upside down.

		(Extend to practise any preposition or adverb. of. inside out: turn a glove, coat, etc. inside out.)
d)	*They'll have to stay* OUTSIDE	Use 'outside' as an adverb and as a preposition. Also practise 'inside',

> Look out of the window. Tell me what's happening outside.
> Is there anyone outside the door? Go and look (outside).
> Leave the room. Stay outside for a minute. Then come back (into the room).
> There's a box on my desk. What's inside (it)? etc.

ii) *people who* BELIEVE IN *us*

Q: Do you believe in ghosts (flying saucers, etc.)?
Do you believe in regular exercise (going to bed early, etc.)?

Relation of the Song to Personal Experience

The main theme of the song is the escape from an unbearable environment (here, the overcrowded city) to find a better life in the country. Ask the class to describe any experience they have had of the unpleasant side of city life. Ask them if they think the picture the singer gives of country life is a realistic one. What drawbacks can they imagine in the 'simple' life (i.e. what are the advantages of city life as opposed to life in the country?).